CASTLE DOUGLAS

Portrait of a Forward Town

CASTLE DOUGLAS
Portrait of a Forward Town

Photographs by Allan Wright
Text by Alistair Livingston

First Published by Allan Wright Photographic June 2016
Second edition published December 2016
www.allanwrightphoto.com

ISBN 978-1-905683-99-4

Design by Allan Wright
Pre print by Small Print, Castle Douglas
Printed in Poland

Classic view from the West of Threave Castle with a regal swim past.

Forword

I chose to live in Galloway 35 years ago, and most days I am reminded that was indeed a good choice. Until recently I lived at Parton, a mere six miles north and so developing an affection for the town was inevitable. Castle Douglas always struck me as a place fit for purpose: practical, well planned and confident by nature, I always knew we were lucky to have it. Earlier this year and with some trepidation, I became a resident. It took a leap of faith to overcome my long held loyalty to abiding as near as possible to wildness and solitude. Life in "The Forward Town" so far has been an engaging journey, and one with plenty unexpected rewards.

Aside from the legendary array of quality shops and the convivial nature of the inhabitants, I am struck by the many walks, short-cuts, nooks and crannies that have revealed themselves to me as I explore my new domain. I have been pleasantly surprised to discover that the town possesses some impressive architectural landmarks. This is coupled with the privilege of having its "shores" lapped by a unique and captivating body of water in the form of the jewel that is Carlingwark Loch.

It was essentially through dog-walking that my eyes and mind were opened to the different layers that compose this cohesive and sure-footed small town. Early morning and later evening sorties fed my growing curiosity and I soon went into full image-hunting mode just as Spring delivered its joyful and colourful expression of the life force. Landscape photography can be a bit solitary but it is also reliably enhanced by chance encounters with like-minded people who are also out walking, usually for the simple, meditative pleasure of it. These are often people with whom I have shared the moment. I love to hear about what interests people and what they know about the locality - real people in real time, almost always uplifting. In this regard I have enjoyed many such encounters. My companion during many of these walks has been a formerly rampaging country-schooled Labrador, who also seems to have learned manners and taken to town life with relative ease.

I have sussed out and savoured numerous views on offer from the surrounding gentle hills and gaps between trees and buildings that surround the town. I have taken delight also in how on the outskirts, both the agricultural lands and the wilder habitats merge into the dwelling spaces in a respectful way. I believe kids growing up here are most fortunate in having real countryside to grow up in. Its feels like one of the most valuable things I can recall from my own childhood experience.

Photography is mostly about seeing; all that "techy" stuff is very much secondary. One of the great joys I found whilst putting this work together has been a renewed sense of communion with nature. The everyday semi-wild habitats on the doorstep are uplifting, surprising even, but also a connection with nature of human kind. Both of these accompany me when I am delving into new territory - it becomes a sort of mobile meditation. As I devised new angles on the town, I relished the way a higher viewpoint elevated the stature of the towers and spires that define and decorate the skylines. I also find it intriguing how places can be immediately recognisable and yet, because of the viewpoint, they appear somehow unfamiliar. It's all about ones' "point of view".

It is with pleasure and privilege I offer this personal exposition of a great little town.

Allan Wright
Castle Douglas
June 2016

Castle Douglas - Portrait of a Forward Town.

Although partially obscured by later developments, the town of Castle Douglas has its origins in the late eighteenth century when landowners across the Scottish Lowlands began to put the Scottish Enlightenment into practice. This origin in the Age of Reason is most clearly seen in the neat grid like pattern of the streets which make up the town centre. The main street, King Street, runs smoothly down from the Market Hill to Carlingwark Loch, flanked on either side by Queen Street and Cotton Street. The three main streets are then connected and dissected by Market Street, Academy Street, Church Street and St Andrew Street. This symmetrical pattern was created for Sir William Douglas who founded and gave his name to the town in 1792.

Douglas, who along with his brothers, had made his fortune as a merchant trading with Virginia and the West Indies, bought the land the town now stands on for £14,000 from Sir Alexander Gordon of Greenlaw in 1789. Gordon's mansion house still stands, overlooking the Stewartry Rugby Club's grounds half a mile to the north of Castle Douglas.

Following the Scottish Reformation, by the beginning of the seventeenth century Gordon's family had managed to acquire virtually the whole parish of Crossmichael which had previously belonged to Lincluden Abbey near Dumfries. Even after some of the lands had been sold off, the Gordon's still owned a large part of the parish. Keen to improve his inheritance, in 1765 Alexander Gordon had a short stretch of canal cut linking Carlingwark Loch with the River Dee. Gordon had discovered, probably in 1764 when part of the Old Military Road was being constructed nearby, that there were beds of shell-marl, a lime rich clay, in the loch. By spreading the marl on their fields, landowners could dramatically increase crop yields.

As well as making it easier to transport marl from the loch to his lands, Gordon was also able to sell the marl to farmers along the Dee/Ken river system as far north as the head of Loch Ken 15 miles away. Unfortunately, Gordon had also invested most of his family fortune in the Ayr Bank. When this collapsed in 1772, Gordon was unable to carry through his ambitious plans for further improvements. These included extending his canal south towards the sea at Kirkcudbright and north to the Dalmellington coal field. Gordon had also planned to create a new town beside Carlingwark Loch.

In 1787, William Cunningham, a Glasgow tobacco baron who had recently bought Duchrae (now Hensol) estate in Balmaghie parish visited Alexander Gordon. Gordon showed Cunningham the marl working at Carlingwark and the houses he had built for the marl workers. After informing Cunningham that he hoped to make Carlingwark village into a Burgh of Barony, Gordon tried to interest Cunningham in buying the loch and 400 acres of adjacent ground which he wished to sell 'being much involved in debt and having a large family.' Cunningham declined the offer, but in 1789, William Douglas accepted.

To keep his new canal supplied with water, Gordon had a cut made through Carlingwark Hill into Carlingwark Loch. This reduced the level of the loch by about 8 feet and revealed the remains of mysterious wooden buildings in the loch. We now know that at least one of these structures was a crannog, a wooden roundhouse built on an artificial island. By 1840, Gordon's canal and marl works had fallen out of use and the level of the loch was allowed to rise again, but Ash Island in the south of the loch marks the crannog site.

In 1868, two fishermen managed to haul a bronze cauldron up out of the loch near Ash Island, in the cauldron were of 100 pieces of metal work. Although most are of native Iron Age origin, a few are Roman, including scythe blade and chain mail fragments. The Roman metal work connects Carlingwark Loch with a sequence of Roman forts and marching camps discovered by aerial photography at Glenlochar two miles away. The cauldron and its contents are therefore most likely to have been place in the loch as a religious offering to a 'lady of the lake' sometime around AD 100.

Along with the two Neolithic standing stones which can be seen in a field below the Urr Valley Hotel, the pre-Roman Pony Cap found on Torrs farm nearby and some Bronze Age cup and ring markings on Threave Estate, it is clear that the area in and around present day Castle Douglas has a history of human settlement stretching back several thousand years.

The most dramatic link with the past is provided by Threave Castle. This was built for Archibald the Grim after he became Lord of Galloway in 1369. Archibald was an illegitimate son of James Douglas, Robert Bruce's most loyal companion. However, during the Wars of Scottish Independence, Galloway supported the Balliol family rather than the Bruces. King John Balliol and his son Edward, who both claimed the Scottish Crown, traced their ancestry back through Devorgilla (who founded Sweetheart Abbey) to her father Alan of Galloway and ultimately to Fergus who ruled Galloway as an independent kingdom until deposed by the Scots in 1160.

Even after Edward Balliol died in 1365, Galloway's Gaelic clans resisted David II's rule. However, once Archibald's castle on Threave Island had been constructed the 'wild men of Galloway' had little choice but to accept his rule. But by 1455, the power of the Douglas family had become a threat to James II. In the summer of 1455 he besieged the castle. Its defenders held out for several weeks before, probably through bribery, they were persuaded to surrender. The castle was besieged again in the summer of 1640, when it was held for Charles I against the 'Army of the Covenant'. In September Charles gave the defenders permission to surrender, which they did.

In 1855, John Nicholson of Kirkcudbright published the Minute Book of the War Committee of the Covenanters. This shows that on 14 October 1640 the War Committee met at Threave where they ordered that Archibald's the Grim's great castle should be put out of commission. The exact words recorded are that:

The sklait roofe of the hows and batlement thereof be taken downe with the lofting thairof, dores and windows of the samen and the hail iron worke of the said hows.

At the same meeting it was agreed that Robert McLellan of Barscobe in Balmacellan parish could purchase the best of the 'freistane' from the castle. McLellan need the stone to improve his tower house. The gaping holes in the stout walls of Threave result from McLellan's work rather than, as legend has it, damage caused by Mons Meg during the siege of 1455. Elaborated by Joseph Train in 1829, this tale states that the great cannon Mons Meg, now a feature of Edinburgh Castle, was built by a blacksmith called Brawny Kim at the Buchan on the edge of Carlingwark Loch in 1455.

Train, who is celebrated by a memorial in Castle Douglas Town Hall, is best known as an antiquarian who provided Sir Walter Scott with material for 'Old Mortality' and 'The Heart of Midlothian'. In 1850 Charles Dickens visited Castle Douglas to meet Train who was then living in retirement at Lochvale House on St Andrew Street.

In reality, Mons Meg was built at Mons in Flanders in 1449 as a gift for James II. It was not built in Castle Douglas… However, at the time of the second siege of Threave Castle in 1640, the Buchancroft was occupied by a blacksmith called Adam McMin. McMin's father-in-law Thomas Hutton was a member of the War Committee of the Covenant. It is possible that Adam forge at the Buchan was used to repair cannons used in the siege of Threave Castle, thus providing a source for the later legend. The McMins were a well known family of blacksmiths. In 1724, Francis McMin joined the Galloway Levellers and was alleged to have killed some Irish cattle seized by the Levellers using his blacksmith's hammer.

In peacetime, Thomas Hutton of Arkland farm in Kelton parish also owned an inn on Carlingwark Hill. In 1635 Hutton's inn was recommended to travellers passing from Carlisle to Portpatrick. It was this traditional route to Ireland that was improved in 1764/5 to create what is now the Old Military Road. The road was designed for soldiers on the march, not horses and carts. Then in 1801, Ireland became part of the United Kingdom which led to the construction of a new turnpike road from Gretna to Portpatrick. Although the new road twisted and turned to avoid steep hills, it did pass through the new town of Castle Douglas. Other turnpike roads, including one from Castle Douglas to Ayr, connected the Portpatrick road, and with it Castle Douglas, to neighbouring towns and the surrounding countryside.

As the nineteenth century dawned then, Castle Douglas began to grow, its prosperity stimulated by the stage coaches, mail coaches, four wheeled wagons and droves of cattle and sheep which could now easily reach the town. Soon the traditional horse and cattle fairs which had been held on Kelton Hill and at Rhonehouse on the Old Military Road gave way to weekly livestock marts held every Monday on the Market Hill in Castle Douglas. Even the centuries old midsummer fair held on Kelton Hill, which had become notorious for drunkenness and petty-crime, passed over into history.

By 1841 Castle Douglas had a population of 1848 including bankers, doctors, solicitors, shop-keepers, cabinet makers, tailors, masons, joiners, blacksmiths, painters, shoe-makers, inn-keepers and labourers. The shops in the town were described in 1844 as being 'remarkably elegant and well-furnished, so as to awaken the surprise of strangers who are not aware that the town is the Mart not only of the parish of Kelton but the whole Stewartry of Kirkcudbright.'

While Kirkcudbright retained its status as the administrative and legal centre for the Stewartry, Castle Douglas became the district's pre-eminent commercial centre. This status was confirmed when the Victorian railway system reached Galloway. Castle Douglas was linked by railway to Dumfries in 1859 and to Stranraer in 1861. Kirkcudbright had to make do with a branch line from Castle Douglas which was opened in 1864.

The coming of the railway left its mark on the architectural fabric of the town. Castle Douglas Town Hall was built in 1862 using sandstone brought by train from Locharbriggs near Dumfries. The Royal Bank of Scotland on King Street (originally the National Bank of Scotland) was built in 1864 using granite from Dalbeattie. To begin with the railway station lay outside the town, with King Street only reaching as far up as the Market Hill. Within 30 years, the town had grown to embrace the station and the increase in prosperity the railway brought can be seen in the imposing villas built along what is now Ernespie Road beyond the station.

The Dumfries to Stranraer railway and the branch line to Kirkcudbright were closed in 1965. Although Dr Beeching's 1963 report found that Castle Douglas was a profitable station for both passenger and freight traffic, the introduction of roll on/ roll off ferries between Stranraer and the north of Ireland had seen a shift from rail to road traffic. As more and more cars and lorries used the A 75, the justification for keeping the Dumfries to Stranraer railway open diminished.

While the network of roads which had helped Castle Douglas grow before the railway arrived continued to serve the town after it had gone, by the 1980s 'ferry traffic' on the A 75, which still passed through the town, was becoming a major problem. The solution was the Castle Douglas By-pass which was built in 1988. Half way along the by-pass it crosses Alexander Gordon's canal at the same point where the Kirkcudbright railway (now a footpath to Threave Estate) crossed the canal. Despite some fears at the time, the by-pass did not lead to a decline in the town's fortunes. Instead, by reducing the heavy freight traffic passing through the town, it made Castle Douglas a more attractive place to spend time shopping in.

The main shopping street is, as it always has been, King Street. In 1976, Jean Gibson wrote a town guide which listed 62 of the businesses then trading on King Street. In 2005 there were 124 businesses trading on King Street of which 19 had been trading in 1976. Of the businesses surveyed in 2005, about 30% were either new since 2000 or had changed ownership. So while a core of businesses have provided continuity on King Street since 1976, the overall pattern is one of progressive change. As one shop has closed, another has taken its place, with only a few lying vacant for any length of time.

This is quite a remarkable achievement, since over the same period, a shift to out of town shopping has seen High Streets across Britain falling into decay and decline. It is a tribute to Castle Douglas that the town has bucked this trend so it still has butchers, bakers, cabinet-makers and many other successful businesses trading in the town centre.

Castle Douglas is a town which while appearing to be a typical, traditional, rural market town has managed to keep re-inventing itself over the past 200 years. When imported lime replaced marl from Carlingwark Loch soon after the town was founded, Sir William Douglas was able to establish a cotton weaving business to take its place. When weaving became mechanised, the cotton factory closed in 1831, leaving only Cotton Street to mark its passing. No longer an industrial centre, the town re-invented itself as the commercial and business centre of the Stewartry of Kirkcudbright. One of the businesses which dates from this pre-railway era is Wallets Mart, founded in 1857 by livestock trader Thomas Wallet.

When the age of the stage coach was brought to an end by the railways, the town grew to meet the new challenge. For a hundred years Castle Douglas goods yard was a hive of activity, acting as a distribution and reception hub for incoming manufactured goods and outgoing agricultural produce. But by the time the railway vanished, the town had already moved on, having long since adapted to the internal combustion engine.

By-passed in 1988, the town re-invented itself again, offering visitors a traditional seeming alternative to USA style shopping malls through the range and diversity of shops on King Street with the added advantage of free parking… At the same time, the central location of the town not just within the Stewartry but within Dumfries and Galloway continued to benefit 'bankers, doctors, solicitors, cabinet makers, tailors, masons, joiners, blacksmiths and painters' as it had in 1844. For the 200 or so non-retail businesses based in the town, its central location means they can reach customers and clients across Dumfries and Galloway more easily than they could if based in the larger towns of Stranraer or Dumfries. Castle Douglas is therefore also a central location for region-wide public agencies and commercial organisations to hold meetings, with the added attraction of a chance to fit in some retail therapy.

Most recently, in 2002 Castle Douglas became Scotland's first Food Town. The thinking behind this move was based on the observation that there were over 50 food-focused business based in the town, from the long standing Wallets Mart to the then recently opened Sulwath brewery. The key aim of the Food Town is to encourage visitors (and local residents) to make a connection between the

quality of the local landscape and the quality of the food the same landscape produces. Or put another way, in Castle Douglas you can eat the scenery.

Looking to the future, although the current presence of five empty shops on King Street is a worrying sign, the town's location at a cross-roads between north-south and east-west routes through the Stewartry of Kirkcudbright gives it a geographically strategic significance. Road and railway builders, even a canal maker, have all contributed to the success of Sir William Douglas' planned town. Indeed, of all the 86 planned towns and villages built in Dumfries and Galloway between 1740 and 1830, Castle Douglas has proved the most viable and successful. Whatever challenges the future might bring, history suggests that the town will keep moving 'Forward'.

Alistair Livingston FSAScot, June 2016

Sundown across the water, Carlingwark Loch.

View from top of Screel Hill looking north past Gelston to the Loch and town in the distance.

Midwinter evening and mist gathers rises on the meadows round the town. Viewpoint is the small hillock on Threave Estate overlooking the Castle. There was an Iron Age roundhouse here 2000 years ago.

The classical lines of the Clock Tower backlit by mellow evening light dominates the skyline seen here from a field near the Cottage Hospital.

From the raised ground above the High School, the powerful stronghold of Threave Castle nestles comfortably among the rolling topography of the Dee Valley.

*St John's Church Spire and the Co-op define the location of Carlingwark Street
& Meadow View set among the spring foliage.*

King Street at Dusk.

Sunrise and morning mist streaming through the trees add a touch of the ethereal to the first dog walk of the day, Carlingwark Loch.

The Fullarton, formerly Lochside Theatre in late May & Cherry blossom steals the show in here in Carlingwark Park.

Stormy sky looms dramatically behind Dunmuir Road here at Burghfield Park,
a generous breathing space in the heart of the town. Until closed in 1965, the
railway lines from Stranraer and Kirkcudbright formed a junction here.

Sunset across Carlingwark Loch.

Newly constructed bridge over the canal on one of the many core path encircling the town. Meadow View houses in the distance, this path passes under the A75 heading out to Threave Castle and The Estate.

Nothing characterises the Carlingwark Loch quite like the all familiar "whiteness of swans" gathered at the water's edge.

The freshest of greens and a resplendent Copper Beech decorate the definitive lines of the former St Andrew's Church, now a successful Community Theatre, The Fullarton.

Furbar House and wildflower meadow nestle idyllically at the South West Corner of the Loch at the entrance to Threave Estate. In the summer of 1724 the fine words of the minister of Kelton parish and a bribe of beer and bread from the laird of Kelton saved the dykes at Furbar from demolition by the Galloway Levellers.

The classic lines of the familiar Fullarton Tower compressed against the jewel of the town, Carlingwark Loch.

The natural habitat round the banks of the Loch offer elusive glimpses of town landmarks, here late autumn colours enhance a view from the South West.

Farming is in the blood of the town and prime beef livestock graze contentedly in the fields all around the town and here sunset behind the Glenkens hills marks the end of a perfect spring day.

First cut silage is gathered next to the newly built town Primary School which blends in perfectly with the houses on Brown Crescent & Torrs Drive.

The unique & eye catching hexagonal structure of the Wallets Mart captured in the moonlight. A company founded in 1857 by livestock trader Thomas Wallet, today is a major focal point for the farming community of South West Scotland, attracting livestock buyers from all round the country.

Wallets Marts, sale of Blackface & Scotch Mule Hoggs in Number 1 Ring.

Castle Douglas Golf Course was established in 1904 and is an attractive 9 hole parkland course accessed from Abercromby Road.

The Bowling club is a popular venue.

Core path on the former Kirkcudbright railway, garden shed at Meadow View, Red Kite at Threave Gardens, Douglas Mausoleum at Kelton.

Fred Ballard, Tessera, Enigma, McGill Duncan.

Threave Castle and The River Dee

Threave House, NTS, elegantly set amongst 25 hectares of stunning garden and woodlands also hosts the School of Heritage Gardening.

King Street during the Douglas Day and celebrations.

Rooftop view of the town from the Clocktower.

Our very own fairy tale Castle at Threave, complete with brass bell, charms thousands of visitors each year.

The impressive rude stone tower of Threave is a joy to photograph, often best approached from the West. Romantically shrouded in autumnal mist on this day, it offers up one of its more mellow moods.

The National Trust for Scotland's Threave Gardens are superlative and along with the larger Estate are a stunning asset to the inventory of fine things the town has to offer. The slate urns by artisan stone mason Joe Smith in the Japanese garden are simply exquisite.

Threave's crimson Japanese Acer at the point of "leaf fall" steals the show.

March and a magical morning mist generates an ethereal atmosphere. From the path through the woods behind Threave Gardens heading out to the Estate at large. The town is surrounded and dissected by an extensive network of core paths, a resource of immeasurable value.

It almost seems as if almost every square metre of shoreline on Carlingwark is a visual delight, constantly changing with the seasons and the restlessness of Scottish light.

The sailing school on the Loch is a happy image and so lovely to see nature in synch with such gentle recreation.

Chilly fog descending on a late November day. Alder & Willow trees define the relics of the Crannog structures from ancient times. They are a gift for both image-makers and for those with active imaginations.

A panoramic "big show" of The heart of Threave Estate at precisely the final moments of a rare and magnificent winter's day.

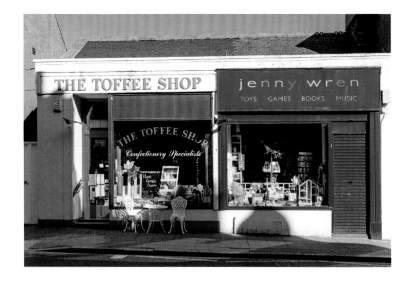

*Toffee Shop & Jenny Wren, Gillespie Gifford & Brown & 501 bus, Deli,
Bengle Tree.*

TAS & McTaggarts (on the site of the engine shed at Castle Douglas station), Meadowpark Stadium, Library, High School.

Midwinter sunset and the unmistakable lines of dominant King Street, the main artery of its retailing power, here positively glowing with an amber radiance.

Moonrise over Carlingwark Loch.

Sunrise over Carlingwark Loch.

Fine style & stone masonry of St. Ninian's Parish Church seen from Carlingwark Caravan Park.

Queen Street, foggy King St, Posthorn, The Crown

Bottom of King Street, Small Print, Douglas House, Market Inn.

Heavy traffic juxtaposed with the striking cross & spire of the Parish Church,
Church Street.

Abercromby Road and familiar skyline shapes rise up to meet the traveller rolling into town from the north on the A713.

Winter and dusk descends across the important Wildlife Reserve of Threave Estate. Islets on the River Dee lie in dreamy unison with the skein of Geese making ragged formations in the sky, gaggling away above the dying embers of the day.

Interpretations of the beloved Threave Castle are limitless. The sweeping lines of these near skeletal ashes in crisp sub zero sunshine were quite captivating.

Big freeze of January 2010 and we get to stroll across the Loch, kicking aside the soft snow in a joyful shuffle whilst revelling in the rare perspective on offer.

The Caravan Park at Carlingwark is immensely popular with scores of devotees returning year after year to recreate in and around the town.

*Livingstons antique restoration & furniture shop and Designs gallery & cafe,
King Street.*

Imperial Hotel, Royal Bank, Marchbank Bakers, Grierson Bros.

Harmonious lines add tranquillity to the deep purple reflections radiating from the gently rippling Loch.